FOR GOD, COUNTRY, AND THE THRILL OF IT

NUMBER ONE
The Charles and Elizabeth Prothro Texas Photography Series

FOR GOD, COUNTRY, AND THE THRILL OF IT

Women Airforce Service Pilots in World War II

PHOTOGRAPHIC PORTRAITS AND TEXT BY

Anne Noggle

WITH AN INTRODUCTION BY DORA DOUGHERTY STROTHER

TEXAS A&M UNIVERSITY PRESS : COLLEGE STATION

Frontispiece: Fifinella, Disney-created emblem of the WASPs

The paper used in this book meets the minimum requirements of the American National Standard for Permanence of Paper for Printed Library Materials, Z39.48-1984. Binding materials have been chosen for durability. ∞

LIBRARY OF CONGRESS CATALOGING-IN-PUBLICATION DATA
Noggle, Anne, 1922–
    For God, country, and the thrill of it: Women Airforce Service Pilots in World War II / by Anne Noggle ; with an introduction by Dora Dougherty Strother. – 1st ed.
       p. cm. – (The Charles and Elizabeth Prothro Texas photography series ; no. 1)
    ISBN 0-89096-401-7 (alk. paper)
    1. Noggle, Anne, 1922–   . 2. World War, 1939–1945–Aerial operations, American.
3. World War, 1939–1945–Personal narratives, American. 4. Air pilots, Military–
United States–Biography. 5. Women's Air Service Pilots (U.S.)–Biography.
I. Title. II. Series.
D790.N64 1990
940.54′4973′092–dc20
[B]   89-20382
                                                CIP

DEDICATION

In honor of the thirty-eight Women Airforce Service Pilots who lost their lives flying for their country in the Army Air Forces during World War II.

Jane Champlin	Dorothy Nichols
Susan P. Clarke	Jeanne L. Norbeck
Margie L. Davis	Margaret C. Oldenburg
Katherine Dussaq	Mabel Rawlinson
Marjorie D. Edwards	Gleanna Roberts
Elizabeth Erickson	Marie Mitchell Robinson
Cornelia Fort	Betty Scott
Frances F. Grimes	Dorothy Scott
Mary Hartson	Margaret J. Seip
Mary H. Howson	Helen Jo Severson
Edith Keene	Ethel Marie Sharon
Kathryn B. Lawrence	Evelyn Sharp
Hazel Ah Ying Lee	Gertrude Thompkins Silver
Paula Loop	Betty P. Stine
Alice Lovejoy	Marion Toevs
Lea Ola McDonald	Mary E. Trebing
Peggy Martin	Mary L. Webster
Virginia Moffatt	Bonnie Jean Welz
Beverly Moses	Betty Taylor Wood

SKY HIGH

The uncommon grace of it
the bulk and the throb.
Flashing in light
we coat the sky with streamers.
unrolling vapors of graffiti
in mock insolence.
I watch the high,
playful
arc of sunlight
dance
across the canopy of my mind.
And even as I sense there is something to be known
it dissolves
like logic unraveling in a dream.

There is movement
I look up at myself
under the helmet
over the mask
through the goggles.
Look at me
I say
Look at me
Riding through eternity.

ANNE NOGGLE, 1970

PREFACE

The ideas for this book came to me in the spring of 1986. Since 1979 when Congress retroactively determined Women Airforce Service Pilots to have been in active military service during World War II, public curiosity suddenly brought us from obscurity into the limelight. Until that time, except among pilots, few knew we had existed. Now that we were established as the country's first women military pilots, everyone seemed to know who we were, but beyond that they had only vague notions of our endeavors. History has a way of depleting the flavor of a time – facts just don't allow for flavor, and anyway, history doesn't involve itself with details.

Physically, I was on an airliner jetting from someplace to another and feeling that gathering knot in my stomach upon takeoff when an old pilot's reaction to the angle of climb warns of an impending stall. It was then I began thinking of how different flying is now, and how glad I am that I flew when any red-blooded aviator tore up the skies without radar and regulations to give caution. Musing in this way brought me to wondering just what made the other thousand or so WASPs take to the skies, as I remembered that before WWII I had known very few women who knew how to fly. Or hardly any men, come to think of it. It wasn't a thing that people just did. Knowing the difficulty it often entailed to obtain parental permission to fly (my grandmother said to my mother, "You just signed her death certificate!"), I wondered if we all perhaps shared similar traits of character that made us go do it. That led to ruminating about how we look today, some forty-odd years later. Could you tell, I smiled, that we came out of the Wild Blue Yonder? At that moment I made up my mind to photograph the WASPs at our next reunion in that coming autumn of 1986, in Sweetwater, Texas.

When I left flying (I could no longer pass the physical examination) after spending a number of years as a flight instructor, airshow pilot, and crop duster, I eventually became a photographer, teaching that subject at the University of New Mexico. Intuition has always played a major role in whatever I do, from liking to fly by the seat of my pants to making portraits with a camera. One of the few women pilots I knew before the war was Dora Dougherty Strother. We have known each other for so long I have forgotten how we met. Dora is probably our most illustrious WASP. Where I came out of the barnstorming aesthetic of the twenties, she with an intellectual curiosity and a scientific bent proceeded up the academic ladder to a Ph.D. with emphasis in aviation psychology. Employed for many years by Bell Helicopters, she was, before her retirement, Manager of Human Factors Engineering and Cockpit Arrangement. Among her many accolades, she was one of only two WASPs checked out in the B-29, our biggest and heaviest bomber during World War II; held women's world helicopter records, which she took from the Russians; was a reserve lieutenant colonel in the Air Force; and recently was inducted into the Texas Women's Hall of Fame. She now is a consultant to Bell and to the Army Science Board.

So here we are, together again in this endeavor. And the similarity between us all? We have all loved airplanes, and the sky in which they truly live. What else? We are all individualists, and we have all put ourselves on the line–and we did it for God, country, and the thrill of it.

ANNE NOGGLE

ACKNOWLEDGMENTS

This is a forty-five-year-old memory. It is as valid in its recollection as any – smudged by the haze of time, made apocryphal by the vagaries of clogged arteries, distorted perhaps by personal vanity, yet true in its essence, in its spirit. At least it is one truth among many.

To history I throw a passing kiss. What I hope to leave by this personal reminiscence is a sense of what it was like to have lived that small drama in World War II.

Thanks to Donald Kuzio for lending me his ear and to Jim Holbrook for his unstinting help and encouragement. Also to the many WASPs who lent me their personal snapshots taken during the war.

FOR GOD, COUNTRY, AND THE THRILL OF IT

WOMEN OF THE *WASP*

AN INTRODUCTION
by Dora Dougherty Strother

The flyers of the Women Airforce Service Pilots (WASP) of World War II were pioneers, the first licensed women pilots in the United States to fly military airplanes for a military service. With enthusiastic response they gladly volunteered when their country asked for help in its time of greatest need.

The WASP was formed in August, 1943, from two earlier, relatively independent programs for women pilots: the Women's Auxiliary Ferrying Squadron (WAFS), an experimental squadron of experienced women pilots employed to ferry aircraft for the Air Transport Command, and the Women's Flying Training Detachment (WFTD), a training program established to supply pilots for the squadron. The intent of the women-pilots programs was (1) to see if women could serve as military pilots, and if so, to form the nucleus of an organization that could be rapidly expanded; (2) to release male pilots for combat; and (3) to decrease the Air Forces' demands on the cream of the manpower pool.[1]

The women initially flew light aircraft on ferry missions, and they soon disproved the negative stereotypes of women as military pilots. They were not too emotional or high-strung. They did not require any more time off than did their male counterparts. Their mechanical aptitude was sufficient to meet the demands of the most sophisticated military flying machines the country produced.

As they performed their first flight assignments in light planes, they proved their capability and stamina. They were then allowed to check out in bigger, faster, and heavier aircraft. Eventually they came to fly every aircraft operated by the Army Air Forces, demon-

---

1. Jacqueline Cochran, "Final Report on Women Pilot Program," Army Air Forces Report 6-1262, Headquarters, AAF, 1945, pp. 3–6.

strating that a woman's hand could guide a fighter plane to a perfect landing as well as any man's.

Their duties included almost all noncombatant stateside missions: ferrying, towing targets for antiaircraft and air-to-air gunnery practice, test flight (including tests of the first American jet pursuit plane, the YP-59A), engineering test flying, flying of antiaircraft drones by remote radio control, flight instruction, smoke laying, administrative flight, and cargo and personnel transport.[2]

The program to use women pilots for military flying began in the summer of 1942, when noted flyer Jacqueline Cochran recruited twenty-five American women pilots to ferry airplanes for the British Air Transport Auxiliary.[3] England was desperately in need of trained pilots. Existing pilot reserves had been drained, and though flight schools were working at full speed, training new pilots took too much time. Women pilots, English and those of the allies as well, were asked to help out.

By mid-1942, the United States, by then deep into the war, was also beginning to suffer similar problems. The losses in the Philippines and the early battles of the Pacific had sapped the reserves of trained pilots. Cochran, who had interested Eleanor Roosevelt in the prospect of using women pilots for military purposes as early as 1939, urged Pentagon brass to establish a training program for ferrying and other missions with some of the three thousand women pilots already flying in the United States.[4] Another experienced pilot, Nancy Harkness Love, whose husband was Deputy Chief of Staff of the Air Transport Command (ATC), also proposed that a small, elite group of highly trained women pilots be used by the ATC to ferry liaison and training aircraft on domestic flights. Both Cochran's and Love's initial proposals were rejected.

2. J. M. England, "Women Pilots with the AAF, 1941–1944," Army Air Forces Historical Studies No. 55, May, 1946, USAF Historical Division, Archives Branch, Maxwell AFB, Ala.

3. Jacqueline Cochran, *The Stars at Noon* (Boston: Little, Brown, 1954), p. 108; England, "Women Pilots," p. 9; Cochran, "Final Report," p. 3.

4. Cochran, "Final Report," pp. 3–4, 7; England, "Women Pilots," pp. 3, 15, 17.

Finally, though, in September, 1942, because the need for pilots was accelerating, the Army Air Forces decided to give women pilots a chance to ferry light planes within the continental limits of the United States, and Love's proposal to employ women as civilian pilots was accepted. To be a member of the WAFS, a woman had to be a U.S. citizen with at least a high school education, had to be between twenty-one and thirty-five years of age and at least sixty inches tall, had to have a commercial pilot's license with a 200-horsepower rating and over five hundred hours of flight time, and had to pass a flight physical and a flight test administered by the Army.

Twenty-five women met those requirements and were hired as civilian employees at $250 per month ($50 less than male civilians hired to do the same work).[5] Love was put in charge of the ferrying activities of all women pilots, and with the first group and later with graduates of Cochran's training program she set up new squadrons of the WAFS at Romulus, Michigan; Dallas, Texas; and Long Beach and Palm Springs, California. She also established detachments at special training bases: Brownsville, Texas, for pursuit aircraft training and Saint Joseph, Missouri, for instrument training.

About the same time the WAFS was organized, Cochran's plans to establish Army flight training of women pilots were implemented, and recruiting began. Over the life of the program, twenty-five thousand women applied for the training.[6]

After initial selections were made, the first class of twenty-eight reported to the Houston, Texas, municipal airport (Howard Hughes Field) on November 17, 1942. The unit, known as the Women's Flying Training Detachment (WFTD), and among themselves as the "Woofteddies," was officially designated the 319th Army Air Forces Flying Training Detachment (AAFFTD).

Already accomplished pilots, the women of the first class of

5. "History of the Air Transport Command: Women Pilots in the Air Transport Command," Historical Branch, Intelligence and Security Division, Air Transport Command [1946].

6. Cochran, "Final Report," p. 1.

the 319th had only slightly less flight time than the five hundred hours required for direct admission to the WAFS. Only a short refresher course was needed to bring them up to the proficiency level required of WAFS pilots. Despite trying conditions in Houston, including their being scattered in boarding houses, motels, and hotels throughout the city, early hours and poor eating facilities that often precluded meals for the entire day, and cold, uncomfortable transportation to the flight line, twenty-three women pilots graduated in the first class at ceremonies held at Ellington Army Air Base on April 24, 1943.[7]

On August 5, 1943, the WAFS and the women of Cochran's WFTD school were united as the Women Airforce Service Pilots (WASP). Cochran was named Director of Women Pilots, and Love continued in the WASP as executive of the Ferrying Division of the Air Transport Command.[8]

Classes entered the WFTD program at monthly intervals. A total of eighteen classes completed training: eight in 1943 and ten in 1944. Of the 25,000 women who applied for flight training, 1,830 were accepted, and of those, 1,074 received their wings.[9] The entrance requirements remained essentially the same as those for the WAFS, except that the age requirement was dropped from twenty-one to eighteen years, and the flight experience requirement was set at only two hundred hours. That requirement was later dropped to thirty-five hours, and the 200-horsepower rating requirement was eventually eliminated.

The second, third, and fourth classes, designated 43-W-2, 43-W-3, and 43-W-4, also entered training in Houston, but in April of 1943 all training was shifted to the 318th AAFFTD at Avenger Field near Sweetwater, Texas. The first classes in Houston flew civilian aircraft that had been taken over by the Army. Gradually, however, military trainers were made available, and the military aircraft were ferried

---

7. Leoti Deaton, "The Gals of Fifinella: A Story of the WASPs," unpublished paper, September, 1976.
8. Cochran, "Final Report," p. 22.
9. Cochran, "Final Report," p. 1.

to Avenger Field by the cadets during the transfer of operations. The first to leave Houston were the primary trainers, ferried by 43-W-4. Class 43-W-3 then ferried the basic trainers a month later, and the second class arrived in Sweetwater in the advanced trainers on May 16, 1943, in time for their own graduation on May 28.[10]

At Avenger Field the women found a class of male cadets training to be transport pilots. The men remained at the field for about two weeks after the women arrived, resulting in the earliest coeducational flight training in the history of the American armed forces.[11]

At first, the female cadets were housed at Bluebonnet Hotel in the town of Sweetwater. Later, they resided at Avenger Field in new barracks that provided for six women to a room, with a foot locker and standing locker for each. There was a small latrine and shower for every two rooms.

Training for the women paralleled but did not duplicate that given male Army Air Forces cadets. Because the women were expected to go into ferrying, emphasis was placed on cross-country flying. Gunnery and formation flight training were omitted. Training time increased as the initial experience of the women pilots entering the course decreased. The first class had received 115 flight hours over five months. By the close of the program the women were receiving seven months' training with a total of 210 flight hours.

Success in flight training was very important to the women, and great emotion accompanied the approach of the end of a phase of training, for it meant a check ride was coming. Looking for any help possible, the women continued a tradition established at Sweetwater by the male trainees who preceded them; on their way to a check ride they would toss coins into a "wishing well," a rock-walled fountain in the center of the barracks area. The well had been altered for the women by the addition of a plaque reading, "To The

10. Deaton, "Gals of Fifinella."
11. "History of the WASP Program, AAF Central Training Command," Historical Section, A-2, AAF Central Flying Command, Randolph Field, Texas, 20 January 1945, p. 46; Faith Buchner Richards to Air Force Museum, subject WASP Class 43-W-4, 1970; Leoti L. Deaton to Dora Strother, December, 1972.

Best Women Pilots In The World, General H. H. 'Hap' Arnold, March 11, 1944." Each cadet prayed that she would be one of those to whom General Arnold had referred.

During the early stages of the program, an 80-percent graduation rate had been anticipated for the women trainees. The actual rates proved to average out at 74 percent for the 1943 graduates and 53 percent for the 1944 classes, the latter actually considerably better than the attrition rate for male trainees in the Central Flying Training Command in 1944. The increase in the washout rates for the women from 1943 to 1944 probably reflected less previous flight experience among the later classes. The women eliminated included not only those dropped for poor flight proficiency but also those with medical and personal problems. The women, unlike the male cadets, because of their civilian status could resign voluntarily.

The WASPs remained employed under the Civil Service program. It was always assumed that they would become a part of the Army when a proper place within the military organization could be found for them, and in fact bills were introduced in Congress to give them military rank, and many of them were sent to an Army Air Forces school to learn how to be officers. Yet even with General Arnold's support of the bills, all efforts to absorb the organization into the military failed.[12]

Nevertheless, the women maintained a military attitude that belied their civilian status. Nancy Love and the women of the WAFS selected gray slacks and a patch-pocket gray jacket as their flight uniform. In the early WFTD classes there had been no standard uniform. Initially, any combination of civilian clothes, except cowboy boots, was allowed. When the flight school moved to Avenger Field, cotton mechanics' coveralls, and later white turbans (called "Urban's turbans" after the 318th's commander at that time), were required wear during duty hours. But soon esprit de corps demanded a professional military appearance. For graduation and dress cere-

12. England, "Women Pilots," pp. 80–87; U.S. Congress, House, Committee on Veterans' Affairs, Select Subcommittee, "Hearings on Granting Veterans' Status to WASPs," 95th Cong., 1st Sess., September 20, 1977, p. 384.

monies the cadets purchased khaki cotton trousers to wear with a white shirt and a khaki overseas cap.

Upon graduation and assignment to their operational units, each flyer bought khaki shirts and trousers for summer flying and Army green or "pink" gabardine for winter. Then in spring of 1944 each woman was issued dress and flight uniforms and flight coveralls of Santiago blue, similar to French ultramarine blue. The dress uniform consisted of a straight, knee-length skirt and a belted coat or jacket worn with either an oxford-cloth blue or white shirt and black tie. The flight uniform was slacks and a short Eisenhower jacket with the blue shirt either open at the neck or with the tie. A beret, pulled to the right, with a gold U.S. coat of arms pinned front and center, was the headgear. Insignia, in addition to the flight wings, included gold lapel wings and pins spelling out "WASP." A black over-the-shoulder purse, black shoes, and gray overcoat completed the outfit.[13]

Of course, like any military-issue clothing, the new uniforms often had to be altered to fit. One base commander with a detachment of WASPs at his field was delighted to hear of the release of the new uniforms and so called a special inspection and review. When the uniforms arrived on the morning of the insepction, all were found to be too large. By exchanging pieces, the twenty-five WASPs thought they could clothe eight or ten women in complete uniforms for the inspection. When the commander heard the predicament, he thought for a moment, then replied: "Well girls—I want *all* of you at inspection. You can solve your problem by pinning the uniforms up in back with clothes pins and safety pins. I will only inspect the front."

Also an object of unit pride was the WASP emblem designed by Walt Disney, who was intrigued with the work of the WASPs. The symbol was a dainty little winged sprite called Fifinella. Fifinella was considered to be a sister of the prank-playing "gremlin" that

13. U.S. Army Air Forces, Headquarters, letter no. AAF 420, AFDQ-3, subject: "WASP Clothing," signed H. R. W. Herwig, Col., Q.M.C., Air Quartermaster.

caused pilots trouble, but unlike her brother, she was a kind-hearted little elf who helped the WASPs out of tight situations.

The flight wings were a special object of individual pride to the women. Those WAFS pilots who went directly in the Ferrying Division of the ATC, though they had not graduated from an Army flight school, wore the wings of the Ferry Division's civilian pilots—wings with a stylized globe and obelisk in the center. Graduates of the first seven classes of women cadets received modified Army pilot wings as a personal gift from Jacqueline Cochran.[14] On these wings the face of the shield was smoothed and the number of the graduating class was engraved on it. Above the shield a scroll carried the number of the flying training detachment, either the 318th or the 319th. Official WASP wings were designed and made available in time for the graduation of Class 43-W-8 on December 17, 1943. In their center was a diamond or lozenge, the traditional heraldic woman's shield.

After receiving their wings, the women pilots of all the classes reported directly to their assigned commands. At their new bases they were checked out on the aircraft they were to fly, and at times they were sent to specialized transition flight courses to learn complex aircraft. One woman, sent to check out on the largest, most powerful pursuit airplane then flying, the Republic P-47 Thunderbolt, was, as might be expected, the only woman in her class. She recalls that she was treated as an intruder until she proved her capabilities by being the fourth pilot in the class to solo. Then she was accepted as "one of the boys."[15]

A dramatic use of women pilots in the Ferry Command is recounted by Lt. Gen. W. H. Tunner. The male ferry pilots were establishing a high accident rate in the hot P-39 pursuit plane. The men called it a "flying coffin." Aware that the men were not flying the plane "according to specifications," Tunner noted that the women pilots "paid attention in class, and they read the characteristics and specifications of the plane they were to fly before they flew it." He

14. Deaton, "Gals of Fifinella," p. 5.
15. Mary Lou Colbert to Dora Strother, undated, in files of Air Force Museum, Dayton, Ohio.

assigned a group of women to check out on P-39s and then to take deliveries on the high-speed aircraft. Sure enough, Tunner writes, "They had no trouble, none at all. And I had no more complaints from the men."[16]

Probably the next job after ferrying in which the women were tested to see if they could perform military flight duties was the towing of antiaircraft targets. The "little black puffs" the WASPs saw around the targets, and sometimes around their aircraft, showed that the ammunition was live and they were playing for keeps.[17]

When the enlisted men on the flight line of the 3rd Tow Target Squadron at Camp Davis, North Carolina, heard that women pilots were coming to learn to tow targets, they all immediately requested transfer. The camp commander asked them to help him train the women and told them he would transfer them as soon as possible. Six weeks later, the story goes, he asked them if they still wanted the transfer, and they replied, "Well, sir, we think maybe we better stick around here and see that these girls get through this damned course."[18]

In many other cases, too, the WASPs not only were proving their capability but also were often being used to demonstrate the safety of aircraft and missions, as they had done with the P-39. Two graduates of the Sweetwater school, Dorothea Johnson Moorman and I, were assigned to check out in the new B-29 Superfortress and then to demonstrate it for training purposes. This new bomber, built especially for the long-range bombing desperately needed in the Pacific theater, was considered a "killer" or a "beast" by the men pilots assigned to train in it. Lt. Col. Paul Tibbets, Jr., later to gain fame as the pilot of the *Enola Gay,* the B-29 that dropped the first atomic bomb, was our check pilot.

We completed our checkout by the end of the third day (de-

16. W. H. Tunner, *Over the Hump* (New York: Duell, Sloan & Pearce, 1964), p. 38.

17. England, "Women Pilots."

18. Charlotte Knight. "She Wears a Pair of Silver Wings." *Air Force,* January, 1944, pp. 49–51.

spite an engine fire during the first flight) and thereafter demonstrated our ship, *Ladybird,* decorated with a painting of Fifinella on the nose, at the very heavy bomber training base at Alamogordo, New Mexico. After a short time, the purpose of the flights had been achieved. The male flight crews, their egos challenged, approached the B-29 with new enthusiasm and found it to be not a beast, but a smooth, delicately rigged, and responsive ship.[19]

WASP Ann Baumgartner, assigned to Fighter Flight Test at Wright Field, Ohio, had a unique experience. She checked out in every fighter and bomber operational during 1943 and 1944 and in addition flew the YP-59A twin-jet pursuit airplane in October, 1944.[20]

Who were the women attracted to the WASP? Their employment before the war had been as varied as that of any similar group of women. They were housewives, mothers, debutantes, students, secretaries, beauticians, flight instructors, and even an actress and a movie stunt woman or two. But their purpose for joining was the same: they wished to serve their country. Some had obvious reasons: Anne McClellan's pilot husband had been missing since the Bataan Death March. Ah Ying ("Hazel") Lee, an American of Chinese ancestry, was engaged to a major in the Chinese Air Force. Some of the women, like twenty-two-year-old Rebecca Edwards, were already widows of the war. Most had husbands, fiances, sweethearts, fathers, or brothers in uniform.[21] No doubt the women loved to fly as much as the male pilots, and some were accused of joining to seek "affairs of the heart." But over and above all other reasons was the feeling that they were making a direct and useful contribution—that they were able to do something for the war effort.

The women of the WASP fulfilled all the expectations of those who initiated the program. They could serve as pilots of military aircraft, releasing male pilots for combat, and their flight performance

19. Aircraft Check Out Form (copy), Dougherty WASP file, AFMR files; Paul Tibbets to Dora Strother, April, 1972, AFMR files.

20. Form 5 Summary (copy), Ann J. Baumgartner Flight Record, Smithsonian Institution, AFMR files; A. B. Carl to Dora Strother, April, 1971, AFMR files.

21. "Girl Pilots," *Life,* July 19, 1943, pp. 73–76.

approximated that of the men in terms of safety and number of available duty days. In total, they flew over sixty million miles in operational flights in every type of aircraft flown by the Army.[22] Thirty-eight of them sacrificed their lives in the service of their country during World War II.

Many accolades and commendations were made to the WASPs. At the graduation of the last class of WASP cadets at Sweetwater, Texas, on December 7, 1944, General Hap Arnold said:

> Frankly, I didn't know in 1941 whether a slip of a young girl could fight the controls of a B-17 in the heavy weather they would naturally encounter in operational flying. Those of us who had been flying for twenty or thirty years knew that flying an airplane was something you do not learn overnight. . . .
>
> Well, now in 1944, more than two years since WASPs first started flying with the Air Forces, we can come to only one conclusion—the entire operation has been a success. It is on the record that women can fly as well as men.
>
> Certainly we haven't been able to build an airplane you can't handle. From AT-6s to B-29s, you have flown them around like veterans. One of the WASPs has even test-flown our new jet plane.
>
> So, on this last graduation day, I salute you and all WASPs. We of the AAF are proud of you; we will never forget our debt to you.[23]

On December 20, 1944, the WASP program was deactivated. The women pilots were told they were no longer needed, that enough men had returned from combat fronts to be able to do their jobs. The legislation in Congress to retain the WASP in the military had failed after encountering a strong opposing lobby from male flight instructors, who became eligible for the draft as their government-contract flight schools closed and who understandably coveted the flight assignments given to the WASP.[24]

22. Cochran, "Final Report," p. 1.
23. R. P. Ward and C. J. Doherty, "History of the 2563d Army Air Forces Base Unit, Avenger Field, Sweetwater, Texas, 1 Nov 1944 to 20 Dec 1944," pp. 94–95.
24. U.S. Congress, House, "Hearings," pp. 204, 239.

The WASPs' lives as military pilots abruptly ended, and they returned to civilian life with no veterans' benefits. For many the transition was not an easy one.

In 1949 the Air Force offered commissions to all former WASPs. One hundred fifteen women accepted these commissions, and twenty-five of them went on to become career officers.[25] Unfortunately, though their commissions were based on their service as WASPs, they were never again allowed to fly military aircraft. Finally, in March of 1979, the Department of the Air Force, in response to Congressional authorization, announced that WASP duty was considered active military service for the purpose of veterans' benefits. The first honorable discharges were presented the following May.[26]

Strong ties of friendship were welded during the trying but exhilarating times when they flew with the Army star on their wings, and since the war the WASPs have met in reunion fourteen times. Each year fewer attend the reunions, and the absent ones are missed. The cofounders are gone now—Nancy Love, founder of the WAFS, died in 1976, and Jacqueline Cochran, the founder and commander of the WASP, in 1980. In 1986, Leoti Deaton of Wichita Falls, Texas —the woman with the title Chief Staff Executive of WASPs, but who acted as the confidante, overseer, and mother superior to all WASP cadets—passed away.

A memorial gathering was held during the 1986 reunion in Sweetwater. After a tribute to all WASPs, living and dead, and to their leaders, the names of those WASPs who lost their lives during the war were read. Every woman present had lost friends. All paused to remember them and to grieve for the bright young lives sacrificed for freedom.

The feelings of the women toward the WAFS and WASP programs, toward their service with the Army Air Forces, toward the aircraft they flew and the jobs they were given, are summed up in the words of WAFS pilot Cornelia Fort, one of the first to volun-

25. Women Airforce Pilots Inc., WASP 1986 roster.
26. U.S. Statutes at Large, vol. 91, pp. 1449–50; Betty Cross, ed., "Women Airforce Service Pilots Newsletter," 18 (March, 1980): 2.

teer when the service was formed and one of those who lost her life in the service. During her few short months as a ferry pilot she wrote:

> As long as our planes fly overhead the skies of America are free and that's what all of us everywhere are fighting for. And that we, in a very small way, are being allowed to help keep that sky free is the most beautiful thing I have ever known.
>
> I, for one, am profoundly grateful that my one talent, my only knowledge, flying, happens to be of use to my country when it is needed. That's all the luck I ever hope to have.[27]

27. "History of the Air Transport Command: Women Pilots," pp. 81–82; Adela Riek Scharr, *Sisters in the Sky,* vol. 1, *The WAFS* (Gerald, Mo.: Patrice Press, 1986), pp. 379–81; Cornelia Fort, "At the Twilight's Last Gleaming," *Woman's Home Companion,* July, 1943, p. 19.

Zoot suits—army-issued coveralls—required during duty hours

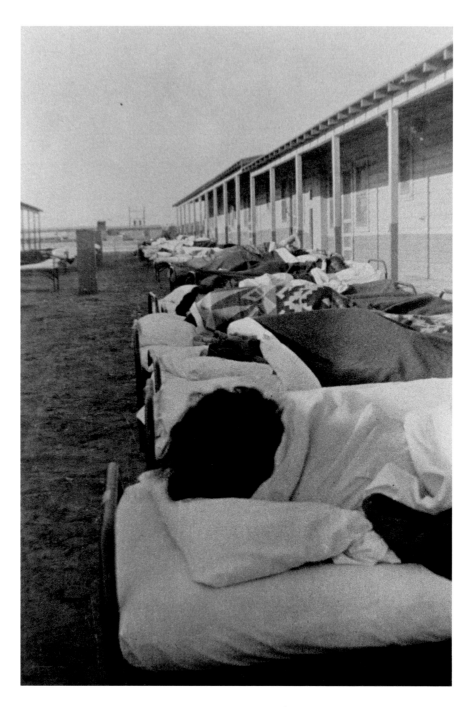

Trainees sleeping outside on a hot summer night

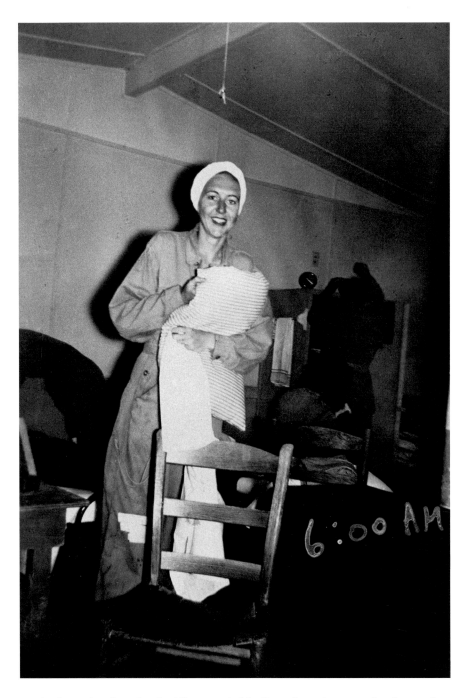

In the barracks changing bedding, probably for a Saturday-morning inspection

Physical training at Avenger Field

Chow line at Avenger Field

Mess hall, showing trainees in Major Urban's turbans

Ground school

Trainees plot a cross-country flight

Trainee filling out form 5 after flight in a Stearman PT-17

A group with their open-cockpit training plane

Going up for solo flight at Avenger Field

Playing airplane for the camera

Trainees paying playful homage to the AT-17, a multi-engine transition aircraft

Trainees in flight gear, showing the short and tall of it

Trainees in primary flight training, standing in front of a Fairchild PT-19

Trainee sitting on the edge of wishing well after being thrown in following soloing

Waiting at auxiliary field for their turn to fly

Weekend respite between barracks, Avenger Field

Civilian clothes, zoot suit, and winter flying gear—left to right

Class of 44-1, flight 2, marching around the wishing well on their way to ground school

Off-duty WASP trainee posing with their intermediate trainer, the Vultee BT-13

Recreation hall on base at Avenger Field

Author as WASP trainee, 1943

Woman pilot flying with her instructor in a North American AT-6 at Avenger Field

A hotshot in her winter flying clothes

The only building on the auxiliary field, Sweetwater

Graduation-day parade on the flight line at Avenger Field (*Army Air Forces photo*)

Jackie Cochran, head of the WASP program, pinning wings on a new graduate
(*Army Air Forces photo*)

Graduating WASPs and Jackie Cochran throwing coins into wishing well (*Army Air Forces photo*)

Saying goodbye to Avenger Field at the front gate

Pilots graduating from Central Instructors School, Basic, Randolph Field, Texas, qualifying them to teach cadets at basic flying schools (*Army Air Forces photo*)

Barracks ready for inspection

Dressing in barracks

The only two WASPs to fly the B-29 standing in front of their plane, "Lady-bird," with aircrew on right and check pilot, Lt. Col. Paul Tibbits (*Army Air Forces photo*)

Dora Dougherty Strother returning from an antiaircraft-target towing mission in a Curtiss A-25

WASP tow pilots on the flight line (*Army Air Forces photo*)

WASP B-17 pilots

WASP in a military plane (*Army Air Forces photo*)

Ferry pilot taking P-63 fighter plane to Alaska to be turned over to Russian pilots
—stenciled on the aircraft: U.S. Army Air Forces USSR (*Army Air Forces photo*)

REMEMBRANCE

I am standing here in Sweetwater, here on what was Avenger Field, here in the wishing well where I was tossed after I soloed forty-five years ago, here physically in my own footsteps with the same sky above, the wind still quick and shifting, the sound of airplanes still here, though with smaller, tighter voices—and yet there is this wrenching in my chest as I fill with remembrance. I try to leave the here and now and make that one journey it is impossible to make—to live it again, not just to relive it. I have returned with my classmates and we collect on the ramp and have our picture taken—we, smiling at one another, in the grace of our friendship, in the ease of our comradeship, knowing our courage but never speaking of it, bonded beyond belief. The class of 44-1. That is how we were known then; that is our mutual identity.

So here is that past, sometimes more real than anything since. Here is a perception of those World War II days when we became the first American women military pilots.

I learned to fly while I was in high school and soloed when I was seventeen. I did much of my early flying at a small airport named Northwest which we all affectionately called Mudwest. The instructors sat around in the office with their feet up on a pot-bellied stove and hangar-talked when they weren't teaching. I propped the airplanes, gassed them, and did the paperwork. Some days I had time only for one swing around the pattern and a landing. The instructors teased me but said my flying was okay, so they almost never rode with me.

Since I wasn't learning maneuvers, I just flew around and looked for something to do. Chicago, being a train center, had tracks coming in from all directions, and I would spot the smoke from the engines and go off to buzz trains. If there were no trains on the horizon, I'd buzz cows. I never had a dual cross-country even though it was required; when I asked the instructors to go with me, they just said, "You can do it," and signed my log book as though they had gone. So I took a road map and flew to Peoria 125 miles to the south. When I wasn't sure where I was, I'd drop down and read the road signs. In this mad, crazy way I built my flying time, and that is how I flew when I was admitted to the flying program at the 318th Army Air Force Flying Training Detachment at Avenger Field, Sweetwater, Texas. If I had been a man flying in those days I would have been described as a wild-ass.

We gathered, my class, in the summer of '43 at Avenger Field in a mishmash of bright summer clothing with our suitcases and a sense of adventure. We were marched, in sandals or high heels, to our newly assigned quarters—six to a bay with a latrine between bays, each trainee given a GI cot and a locker for clothes. We were issued men's olive drab GI coveralls, flight helmet, goggles, a leather flying jacket, and, in the winter, fleece-lined leather pants, jacket, helmet, and flying boots. For dress we were to wear khaki pants and a plain white shirt and a khaki overseas cap. Added to that was an E6B computer for navigation and a stack of books to study for ground school.

Before World War II most of us hadn't been very far from home. I remember a classmate from California who agreed with me that she didn't like the East very well until we discovered she was refer-ring to Sweetwater and I to New York City. I had never been far-ther west and she never farther east than Texas.

For those six months in training we were all as one—eating, studying, flying, and sleeping all in lock step, even thinking similar thoughts, since we were deprived of private time in which to rumi-nate on our own outside worlds. So in this artificial, intense, closely prescribed, off-limits airfield, smack in the middle of West Texas, we coalesced and lived to fly. If I were to describe our attitude at that time with one word, it would have to be *determined*. To be good enough. To earn our wings. We were the isolated experiment, a trib-ute to Jackie Cochran's forceful personality and drive. Most of us were unaware and apolitical, most of us with someone away in the service, doing what needed to be done.

The gate—this was a training base—was the farthest we might wander until the following weekend, when, we were told, if we had no demerits we might leave the base after Saturday morning inspection, or SMI, as they called it, to return late that evening for bed check. Sunday again we were allowed to leave but had to be back earlier in the day.

There was a loudspeaker system, and each morning we awakened to the canned recording of reveille and each night we turned our lights out with taps. We may not have been in the army, but it was hard to tell the difference.

Lots of us worried about check rides, and with good reason. My class started out with about 101 and graduated 49. When someone washed out, they just disappeared, and the only trace of them was the mattress folded over on the cot, waiting to be removed from the bay. Little was said about those who had departed; we just were silent in that empty space for a while. Probably being glad it wasn't us. I never worried about check rides; I had the supreme confidence of my ignorance that it was possible to fail. But my hot-shot pilot ideas almost got me washed out too—I was caught buzzing cows in an AT-6. If they hadn't caught five or six other classmates in the same act a few days later I would have been dismissed—made an example of, they called it—but there were too few of us left, and I suppose we were so close to graduation that they relented. On and off for the rest of my flying career I periodically succumbed to that naughty thrill.

My primary instructor's name was Mitchell, and we flew with me in the front and him in the back seat of an open-cockpit Fairchild primary training plane designated the PT-19A. It was far larger than any aircraft I had flown until then. We wore our helmets, and into mine were plugged two tubes that fit into it on the sides, while he had the other end that he talked into—a one-way conversation, with my response limited to nodding my head in agreement. Yes, I understood; yes, I was not too bright; and on and on.

It turned out my instructor was not well qualified to teach, and they sent him packing and gave me Smitty, a check pilot, as my instructor. I was at that time on takeoffs and landings, and since I'm not as tall as most men, when I would reach down to pull on the flap handle, Smitty would say, "Get your head out of the cockpit!" and I would stop reaching for the flaps and get my head back up. Then again he would order the flaps, and that was how it was on every final approach until I learned to crane my neck and make a no-look swipe at the flap handle and do it too quickly for him to catch me with my head at all down in the cockpit. I caught on to the idea that I had to find everything I needed in the cockpit immediately without looking or with just a glance.

One of my baymates, Marie, had played the flute in the Des Moines Symphony before she came to Texas to fly. She was tall, about six feet, I think, although she looked taller, for she was very straight in posture. I can remember her coming out of the latrine naked and playing the flute. It was quite a sight, and although we were proud of her skills, we soon banished her to the wash house, whence flutey sounds emitted when she practiced.

One day Marie was up in a PT-19 practicing spins with her instructor, and the sleeve of her too-big coveralls, unbeknown to her, caught the seat belt and opened it during a spin recovery. In those planes when you recovered from the spin you pushed the stick forward to the firewall so the nose of the plane really went way under the horizon. When that happened, Marie sailed out over the propeller. Then in her cool and precise manner she pulled the ripcord on her parachute, remembering to hold onto the handle after it released, and floated down into a farmer's field.

When the base sent a vehicle out to recover her, she was apologizing to the farmer for landing on some of his plants and attempting to straighten some of them she had disturbed. It made our whole bay famous for a few hours, and all of 44-1 and gals from other classes came to hear about it and see the ripcord, which she had ceremonially attached to the light cord in the center of our bay. That Saturday everyone in the bay got a demerit for the ripcord—an unauthorized object hanging in our room.

During training our names were, I believe, stenciled on our

coveralls: last name, first name, and middle initial. One of my class-mates was Wood, Carol P., a source of amusement to the rest of us. Shortly before graduation, Carol went on her last long cross-country in an AT-6, which was our advanced trainer, a macho plane with a 650-horsepower Pratt and Whitney engine, a constant-speed propeller, and retractable landing gear—a plane you respected. Carol was flying the leg between El Paso and Tucson when this very bad, fast-moving front passed through the area, and Carol turned up missing. What really happened was that she got lost and made an emergency landing in a tiny field on the side of a mountain miles from Tucson. She landed gear down, and the airplane was okay, not a scratch on it, but there was no way to fly it out because the field was too short. It seems strange that you can get down all right in a field that you then can't fly out of, but it happens.

So Carol got word out where she was and stayed with the aircraft while they tried to locate her from the air, and when a search aircraft found the plane, it circled, but couldn't land. Carol thought the plane wasn't landing because its pilot didn't know which way the wind was coming from, so she ran out into the field and lay down on her back with her arms extended like a wind tee that shows where the wind is, but the plane flew away. A day later a vehicle made it up the mountain to retrieve her. When she was returned to Avenger Field, her parents were already there for our graduation, and she barely made it back in time to get her wings.

The hazards to graduation weren't confined to the flightline. There were regulations to cover everything from our personal appearance and clothing to the arrangement of our lockers. One girl in my flight was nicknamed Demerit because she seemed to have more demerits than most of us, mainly because of bad luck, although there was her famous argument with our flight lieutenant, in which she shouted, "Give me a demerit, give me ten demerits," and so the lieutenant did. Poor Dolores was confined to the base for many weeks. We all had similar problems occasionally, and on a few Saturday nights, sneaking off the base around the end of the runway where a path had been worn by those of us who had erred, I bumped into Dolores leaving the base.

We were not allowed to date our flight instructors. The rules were very specific: be seen with an instructor off the base and you were automatically dismissed from the program. There was no one else in Sweetwater to date. So we dated the instructors—sort of. Some instructor would throw a party and we would go. The town was in a dry county, and we had to go to the bootlegger to buy a pint of whiskey to take with us. In Sweetwater her name was Ma Coleman, and the first time I went to her house and she said, "Come in," I entered and stood looking at her, too paralyzed to speak. Finally she asked me what I wanted, and I squeaked, "Whiskey." With that she lifted one of her ample hips and pulled out a hot pint that she had been sitting on. After that I loved going there.

The pressures on us were tremendous, and we had a schedule that didn't allow us to let down, so when we escaped from the base on weekends, many of us did drink too much, but we took care of one another and everyone seemed to understand the need.

Finally the day came when we graduated and put on the new uniforms designed for the WASP. Neiman-Marcus sent tailors out from Dallas to fit them. They were a rich blue called Santiago. We wore the Air Forces patch on our shoulder, an officer's insignia on our hat, propellers on the lapels, and WASP insignia where the army uniforms wore U.S.

After graduation I was sent to Eagle Pass Army Airfield, where I was assigned to the P-40 Gunnery Squadron as a tow pilot for aerial gunnery.

When I first arrived at the field, right on the Mexican border, there were only a few women tow pilots. Later we did all the towing operations there. In the morning we would fly out to the auxiliary field and fly our missions from there. In the back cockpit we carried a crew member, a tow operator, whose duty it was to let the target out. After it was out, we would call our flight and they would fly a pursuit curve, coming at us from the opposite direction and starting to fire their .30-caliber machine guns at forty-five degrees toward the target and stopping firing at forty-five degrees from our tail. If they did this properly, we would not hear the guns—something to do with the way sound travels. Anyway, we were told that if we heard the guns, they were firing too close to us and we were to inform the gunnery students immediately to stop. The reason was obvious. On and off all day out there on the aircraft radio you could hear urgent feminine voices calling out, "Get off my tail!" There was no time for niceties.

I heard that Edie Keene had been killed when her AT-6 had structural failure and she couldn't get out. Then yet another classmate, Kay Dussaq, went in in bad weather. I don't remember really talking about it among ourselves; we kept busy and we knew there would be losses. I think when you are doing something where there is risk, you don't let it into your conscious mind, at least I didn't. You make a pact with yourself that it might happen but probably not to you, and you are a fatalist—or you quit flying.

We were billeted in a wing of the base hospital designed to hold psychiatric patients, complete with grills on the windows and no door handles on the inside of the rooms. (One of our jokes was to go down the hall shutting every door along the way.) The military never did quite know what to do with us or where to billet us, as we were subject to the Uniform Code of Military Justice yet were civilians in uniform.

I was assigned a new tow operator one day who told me he was totally frightened to fly but his wife had told him he *had* to volunteer because they needed the flight pay. Although he was jittery, he had been through training, so we took off. After some false starts he let the target out all right, and we flew the mission, then returned to the field. In an out-of-the-way area was a white circle where we were supposed to drop the target before landing. I flew over it and told him to drop it. Nothing happened. You could easily tell when the target was released because the plane spurted ahead relieved of its draggy burden. We made a second pass and on and on and it wouldn't release, so I told him to use the huge cable cutters that the operators carried with them as a backup. But he had forgotten the cutters. We came in dragging that target and cable across the scrub behind us, and then it caught the barbed wire fence at the end of the runway and we dragged fence posts, barbed wire, target, and cable all bouncing and clanking behind us.

The stories, which to pilots are known as hangar flying, could go on and on.

There are lots of little things I remember about my classmates. Like how Ikey could clasp her hands together, lean down with them forming a sort of loop, and jump through them without unclasping them. And Dottie, straight out of Rock Springs, Wyoming, asserting herself, sticking up for what was right. She's even more assertive now. We all smile and listen to her, while Doug, her husband who became an airline pilot after the war, smiles the most while she tells us how she feels about whatever it is—but she's 44-1 and loves us as we do her.

Summers in Sweetwater were hot, and we were allowed to move our cots outside between the barracks to sleep under the stars on those nights when the bays were stifling. Phyl and I often whispered after taps about our dreams of the future—she, married to a navy pilot, dreamed of being an actress, and years later in Davenport, Iowa, I saw her star in the road show of *The Voice of the Turtle*.

I think we are becoming more like ourselves every year. Jeanette, our class secretary, becomes more patient with us and mothers us in the newsletter. We don't ourselves communicate so much as we tell Jeanette, and she translates and condenses it and is grateful when we send stamps to her in Ohio to make sure she keeps us together.

Many of us married during the war, and a number of us continued flying for our livelihood. But we could never go back to the way we were. The WASP experience changed us all forever. When I decided it was time to do this book, I wrote a statement about that to the WASPs when asking for their support. I quote from it:

> For a long time I thought about making a photographic document of all of us as we look today. When we met in San Diego for our reunion in 1984, I arrived at registration and while waiting in line I looked and listened and I was filled with the wonderful sense of our vitality, one factor that makes us such a unique group. Then I thought about how few women have had the opportunity not only to fly for our Air Force, but to be thrown together willy-nilly in training and to know the bonding that usually is associated with groups who live and work

in close proximity. This sense of belonging is all the more intense when the duties involve danger and risk. That makes it so rare with women. Add to that the kind of independent women we are and you have a portrait of a Women Airforce Service Pilot. I think we are extraordinary and I decided that I would take, not a group picture, but individual images. I feel that posterity will find these photographs of great interest. We may not be young any longer but we are very much alive.

43-4 Mary Rosso Lewis

44-2 Anne Berry Lesnikowski

44-1 Marie Mountain Clark

WAFS Florence Miller Watson

43-5 Yvonne C. Pateman

43-5 Harriet Urban White

44-2 Lorraine Zillner Rodgers

43-6 Shirley Condit deGonzales

44-4 Ruth Shafer Fleisher

44-5 Jacqueline Twitchell Morgan

43-7 Frances Thompson Hunt

44-6 Suzanne DeLano Parish

44-5 Dorothy Swain Lewis

43-3 Lois Brooks Hailey

44-10 Francie Meisner Park

44-7 Nona Highfill-Holt Pickering

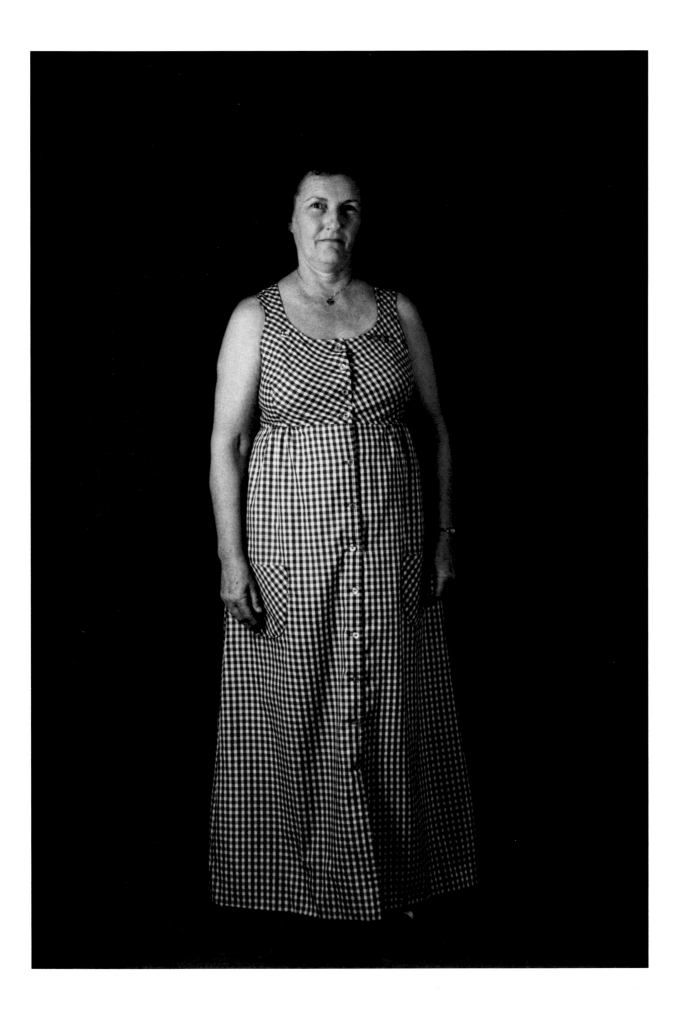

44-7 Bernice Falk Haydu

43-8 Iris Heillman Schupp

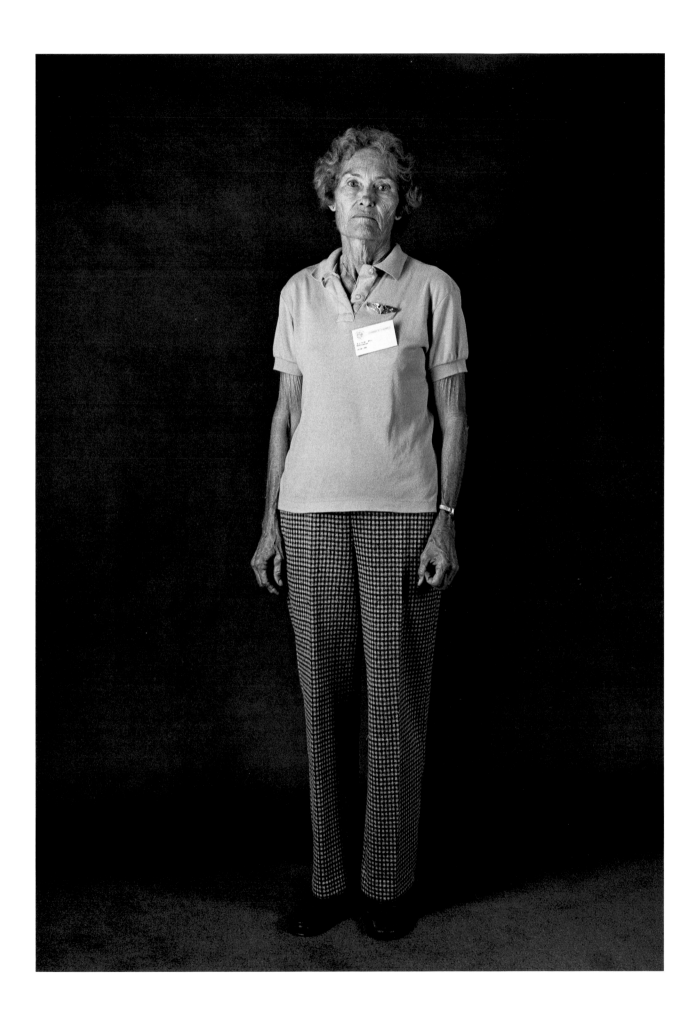

44-1 Eileen Kealy Worden

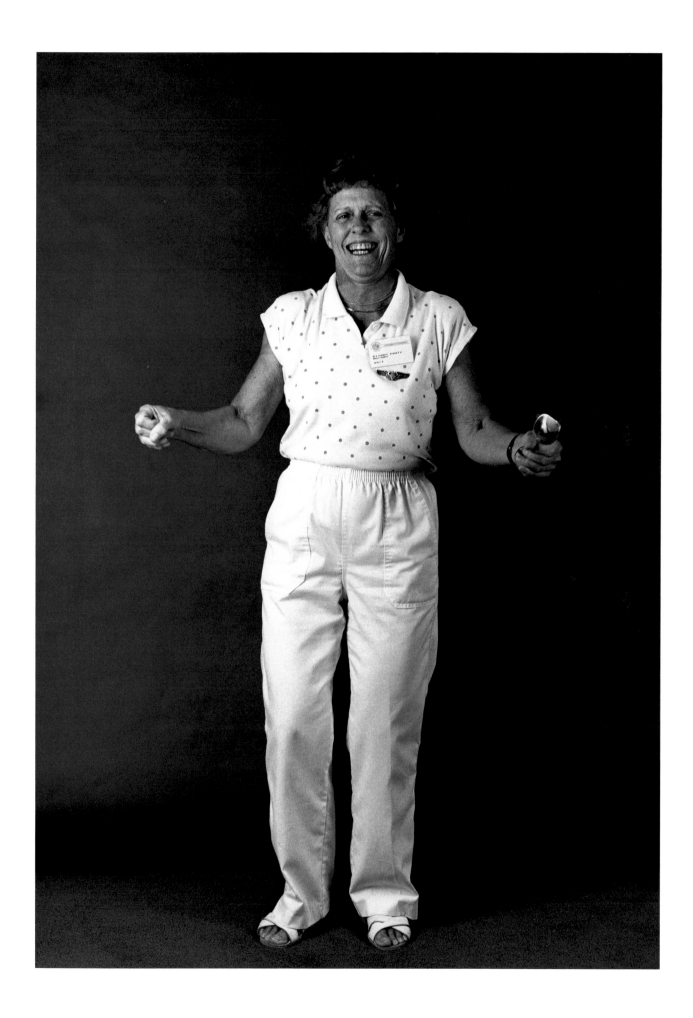

44-8 Marguerite Hughes Killen

44-1 Anne Noggle

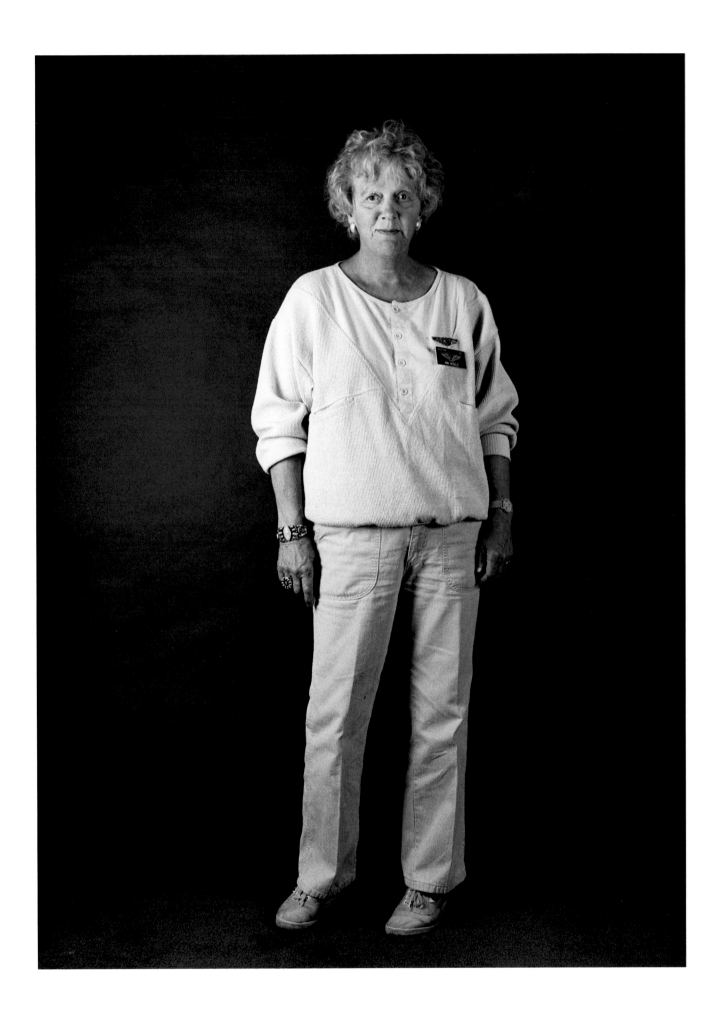

44-6 Dorathea Rexroad Scatena

44-9 Lillian Glezen Wray

44-9 Mary Regalbuto Jones

44-9 Betty Stagg Turner

44-10 Rosa Charlyne Creger

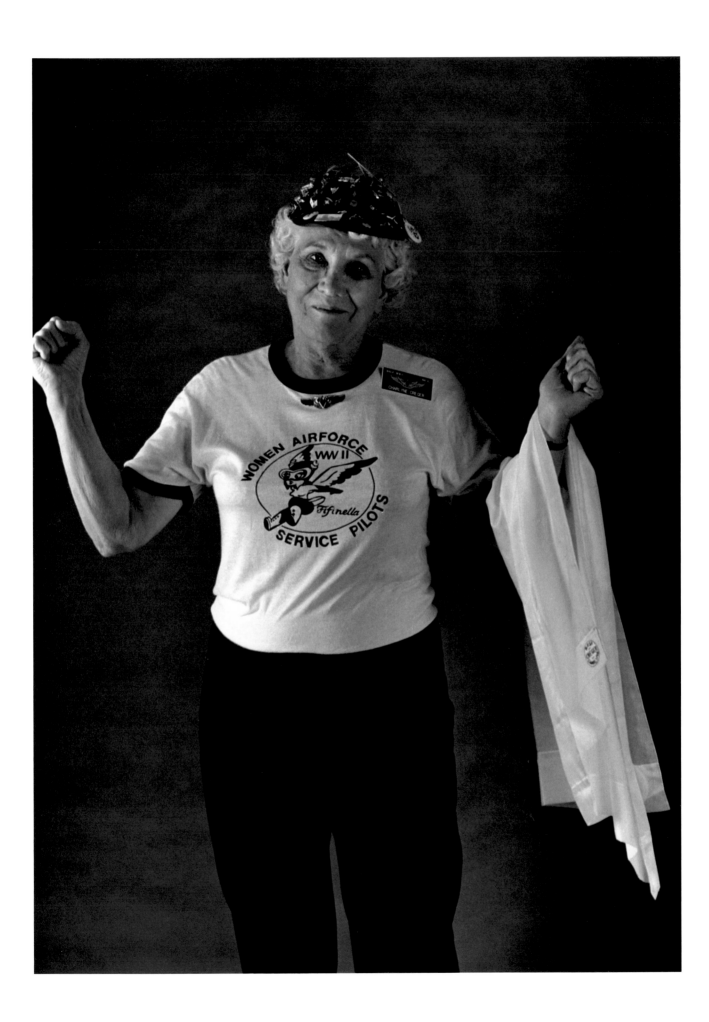

44-9 Betty Martin Riddle

43-3 Dora Dougherty Strother

44-9 Barbara Hershey Tucker

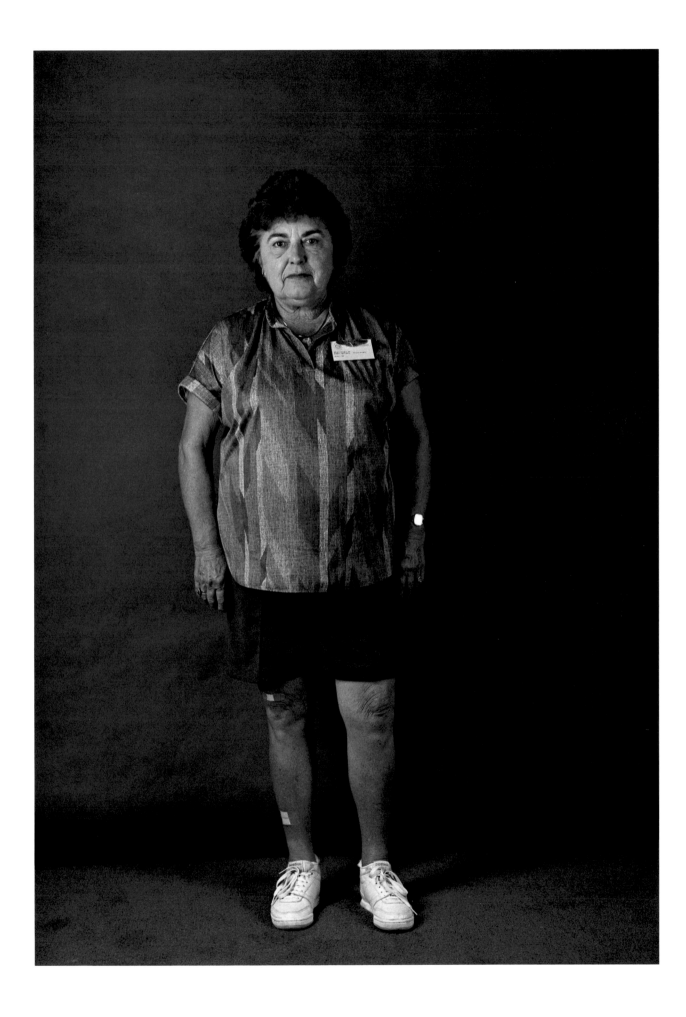

43-3 Joyce Sherwood Secciani

43-4 Violet Thurn Cowden

43-6 Evelyn L. Trammell

43-8 Mary Estill Fearey

44-9 Elizabeth Briscoe Stone

43-7 Yvonne Ashcraft Wood

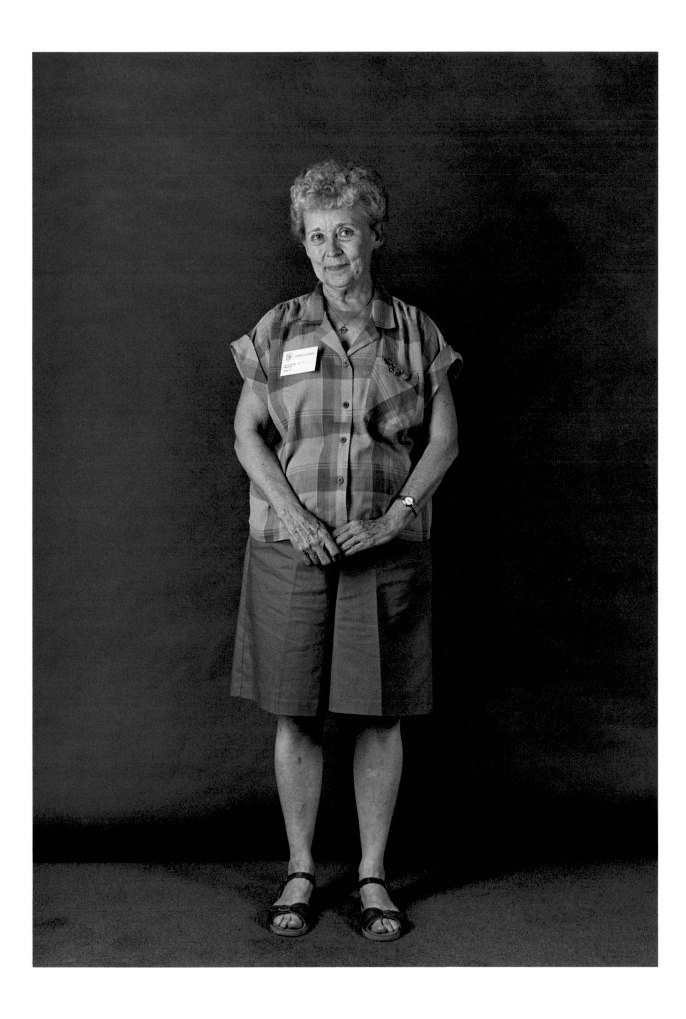

44-9 Janet Wayne Tuch

44-5 Alma Newsom Fornal

44-2 Kate Lee Harris Adams

43-4 Helen M. Schaefer

43-5 Hazel Armstrong Turner

44-7 Geraldine Bowen Olinger

44-1 Ida F. Carter

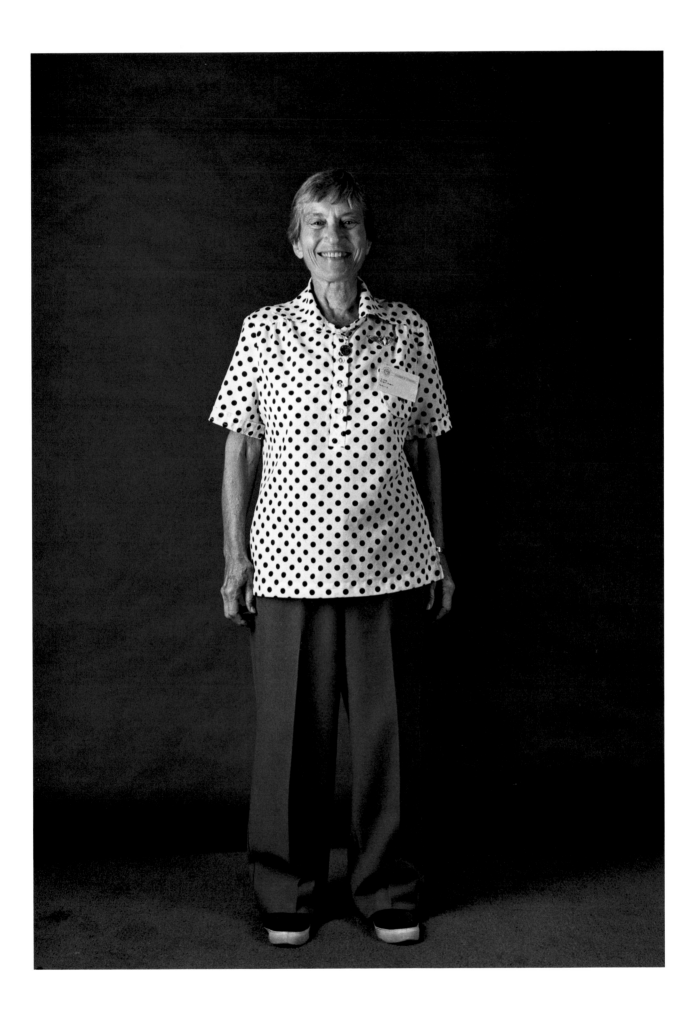

44-7 Joan Smythe McKesson

44-4 Grey Allison Hoyt Dunlap

44-6 Mary Retick Wells

44-8 Pearl Brummett Judd

44-6 Shirley Chase Kruse

44-8 Bonnie Dorsey Shinski

For God, Country, and the Thrill of It was composed into type on a Compugraphic digital phototypesetter in twelve point Galliard with three points of spacing between the lines. Galliard was also selected for display. The book was designed by Jim Billingsley, typeset by Metricomp, Inc., and printed offset by Meriden-Stinehour Press. The paper on which this book is printed bears acid-free characteristics for an effective life of at least three hundred years.

TEXAS A&M UNIVERSITY PRESS : COLLEGE STATION